Tidal Fury

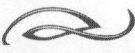

Brenda Clews

ESSENTIAL POETS SERIES 238

Canada Council **Conseil des Arts**
for the Arts **du Canada**

ONTARIO ARTS COUNCIL
CONSEIL DES ARTS DE L'ONTARIO

an Ontario government agency ·
un organisme du gouvernement de l'Ontario

Canadä

Guernica Editions Inc. acknowledges the support of the Canada Council
for the Arts and the Ontario Arts Council. The Ontario Arts Council
is an agency of the Government of Ontario.

We acknowledge the financial support of the Government of Canada.
Nous reconnaissons l'appui financier du gouvernement du Canada.

Tidal Fury

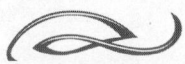

Brenda Clews

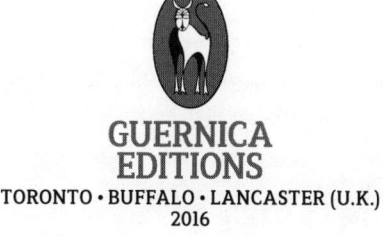

GUERNICA
EDITIONS
TORONTO · BUFFALO · LANCASTER (U.K.)
2016

Michael Mirolla, editor
Cover design, Allen Jomoc Jr.
Interior design, David Moratto
Cover and interior images, Brenda Clews
Guernica Editions Inc.
1569 Heritage Way, Oakville, (ON), Canada L6M 2Z7
2250 Military Road, Tonawanda, N.Y. 14150-6000 U.S.A.
www.guernicaeditions.com

Distributors:
University of Toronto Press Distribution,
5201 Dufferin Street, Toronto (ON), Canada M3H 5T8
Gazelle Book Services, White Cross Mills, High Town, Lancaster LA1 4XS U.K.

First edition.
Printed in Canada.

Legal Deposit—Third Quarter
Library of Congress Catalog Card Number: 2016938888
Library and Archives Canada Cataloguing in Publication
Clews, Brenda, author
Tidal fury / Brenda Clews. -- First edition.
(Essential poets series ; 238)
Poems.
Issued in print and electronic formats.
ISBN 978-1-77183-099-7 (paperback).--ISBN 978-1-77183-100-0 (epub).--
ISBN 978-1-77183-101-7 (mobi)
I. Title. II. Series: Essential poets series ; 238
PS8605.L544T54 2016   C811'.6   C2016-902176-9   C2016-902177-7

Contents

∽

Tidal Fury

Brenda Clews

～ Entrap*

The sky, trapped in clouds,
threatening; air, heavy with words,
the weight of droplets
that sleet earthwards,
crystals breaking on pavements,
streaming on windows.

The day, steamy, damp. I tap on a laptop by the window of an Italian café
sipping a cappuccino. I write to *him*.

An obscure woman attacks my writing as impenetrable. Her target was
someone else. The arrows, the marks. The woman, haunting, her odd
responses, the ceaselessness of her words.

Monsieur, does the writing we are immersed in trouble you? The
communities I post in, flocks of birds flying in scattered formations. Today,
mon cher, I am not good with words.

Describe her? I trace patterns in her words, reading her braille of air. We
surf where the screen becomes a brine of glass and posts open and close
like visions, where writing is an ocean continually closing over itself.

Her stories, long, drawn out; paragraphs encroach. Waves dissolve sand,
the shore. She is a rising tide, it overwhelms. My screen splashes spilling
breakers.

Imagine her? Her hair like seaweed, pulled back loosely with wisps lining
the face. I've never seen her, or gazed at a photograph. She wears veils of
words, obscuring sea sprays of forcefulness that surprise.

I use the imagery of water, *Monsieur*,
but the metaphors shift and leave the desolate
shore and come into the city of words,
to her house, where she moves
like an exotic figment, a flash of fabric and skin.

She rustles, a blackness of cloth, and red—rhinestone-glint brooch of a
poppy; toss of beaded rose earrings, like Native American dream catchers;
or that ruby rising out of a ring of melted, cast sun, on hands woven with
pale veins and the delicacy of a musician's fingers.

Open her closet. On the floor, red canvas tennis shoes, ginger petal satin Chinese slippers, patent leather ruby heels, flaming red slick knee-high boots. On the shelf, a vinyl scarlet belt, crimson silk sash, red opera gloves, a vermilion felt hat. Dragging down the white wall like Barnett Newman's "Lema Sabachthani" series, a funerary dirge of black dresses, a heavy curtain of silk, cotton, corduroy, rayon, wool hung on shellacked cedar hangers.

Her unkempt garden teems with the untended, un-weeded, like writing that chokes. Think of musty split pomegranates decaying. And Beardsley's version of Oscar Wilde's "Salomé," drawn in black lines, but aged, with white skin, black habit, and the blood-red splashes that are uniquely hers. Florid perfume and compost: her writing resembles a mass of cut flowers in varying stages, some dying, some bursting forth; floral, with dark passion.

Salt swirls, leeches the soil. Dying follows her. She's in a difficult economic situation. How she came to penury is a tale that grows stranger with each telling. The publications for which she wrote were autumnal leaves that fell and floated away. Her fish bones were broken and reset crookedly. Yet she fishes, and scales mercilessly what's caught. Is she a victim? Or a perpetrator? I don't know.

Are there any true stories?

An onrush of waves, from the sky, the ocean. Sea water spills in my mouth. Monsieur, I beseech you, help me break free of the undertow. Why does she silence us—I, and the others? She speaks in the diminutive. Sarcasm of a seaward parrot, words twisted in the ruffle of virid and cinnabar feathers, inside the sharp beak. Have I found someone to beleaguer my laboured writing? Unbearable, the denouncer's voice. For a fertile slope, my Sisyphean ball of letters, instead of this ocean of caustic words. Can't I turn and go elsewhere, where welcomes wait?

Monsieur.

Your beloved.

---

* Entrap: allure, beguile, benet, box in, catch, decoy, embroil, enmesh, ensnare, entangle, entice, hook, implicate, inveigle, involve, lay for, lead on, lure net, reel in, rope in, seduce, set up, snare, suck in, tempt, trap, trick
Antonyms: clear, free, liberate, release
Roget's Thesaurus : http://thesaurus.reference.com/browse/entrap

➤ Clipped

A sea of turbulent words, *la mer*. I know this woman who is a stranger. I read my past into her, *Monsieur*, and I ask how to stop when the *virid*, the *cinnabar*. I am under wing.

Clipped.

When she imagines insects rising from a hole in my belly and she screams. When she cannot forget.

When I am deprived of the power of speaking.

➤ Undercover

Your writing draws me in, Monsieur. You breathe words into me, hot, intimate. I slip under the covers of those words, where langue pulsates, where lives are assembled, dissembled and reassembled, where poetry is born.

Connecting, interlacing, the pulsing energy where we fall in love, are enrapt.

➤ Polarity

I cannot not struggle with words.

Why is it easy to constrict the writing voice? With harsh criticism, the shivering.

The bed is delineated and unkempt. They prefer opposite sides. A 'talking head' and the simmering passion of angst and deep meditation on the paradoxes, ambiguities and fleetingness of life, love. Can we extrude these polarities?

The bed floats in the void. White sheets against darkness. One side, cold and still; the other, inflamed and sliding away. The critic tabulates, clutching the fingers of poetic impulse, or lets them fall away.

Singed wing of an angel.

❧ Conjunctions

Mon cher, I imagine you, baggy, paint-splattered shirt, stripping walls, sanding wainscoting and baseboards, smoothly slapping colours from soft, entrained bristles to walls, layers covering the inside of your house, stopping to rest by the ladder, standing, breathing the latex fumes, your speckled canvas runners on the speckled floor of protective canvas, thinking of your life, women, the meaning of the conjunctions in the stars.

You're painting your walls *virid* green and *cinnabar* red.

❧ Sweet Life

The only man, *un autore*, who speaks of love in the film shoots those he loves most at close range, his children behind white billowing diaphanous curtains, then, seated in his black leather armchair, in his black suit, himself.

We should learn to love each other so much we live outside time ... detached.

He said (Steiner). *La Dolce Vita* (1960).

Who can love in a world where money must be made? The film is from a man's perspective. It is the women who talk of love, if love is spoken of —especially Marcello's fierce, suicidal and beautiful girlfriend for whom love is possessive.

Those whose lives overflow with money don't know what to do with love either. Fellini knows this. Love wants to hold, to keep forever in its embrace, but it's all feathers. The clouds of pillows become unstuffed. We are tarred with our desires. What we are searching for are endings.

∾ Hybrid

She finds seagull feathers. She tars my words.

Dead eyes watch us. The flat hybrid monstrous fish on the beach at the end of *La Dolce Vita*. She sent it to silence us.

To take our words into its mouth; to be swallowed.

∾ Unravelling

Words fly from the edges of clouds fleeing the sky, unraveling.

Airborne texts, secret sky writing, *dakini* decrees; it could be loose feathers. Or the luminescence of angels fleeing a sky they never leave.

The birds fly in a V- formation and swirl chaotically, joining the others who fly in random circular orbits. Who feeds them? Feathers fall to earth: white, grey, black; some are *cinnabar* and *virid*.

∿ *Unblinking Eye*

We are filmed, in the store, at the bank, on the street. It never stops.

The eye that doesn't weep, the unblinking eye, dangerous. Warhol's unblinking eye. In his Factory studio, a camera continuously filmed the corner, where the black couch was. In the clips we see a gyrating naked woman, her breasts, their pale veins, the nipples, in the light, pubic hair disappearing into the crux, her undulating hips; the man polishes his motorcycle without noticing her. Or the naked men, one lying on top of the other, humping for hours while someone moves in front, sweeps the floor, and the man polishes his motorcycle. No-one cares, or watches. Only the unblinking eye, continually filming.

The unblinking eye, without ethic.

Perhaps the eye that weeps finds pathos, ethos.

And do we find ourselves weeping before the accident victims Warhol blew up from newspaper images into wall-sized silk-screen repeating images that fade out? Who are the anonymous dead people? Without the narrative of their lives, they are anyone, us. We gaze; we do not weep.

∾ *Braille*

Monsieur, you are a figment. I gaze on you
blindly. Without sight, scent, feel. Only your
words massage my throat, my breasts.

I write you into my book because
you are here.

Writing is blind.

Marks on the page. We intuit
the contours. Memoirs of an
imaginal life. After I lost
my sight, I could see. I drew
a calligraphy of letters,
a Braille of seeing.

These lines are
not visible. Read
them to me now.

Braille

Monsieur, you are a figment. I gaze on you
blindly. Without sight, scent, feel. Only your
words massage my throat, my breasts.

I write you into my book because
you are here.

Writing is blind.

Marks on the page. We intuit
the contours. Memoirs of an
imaginal life. After I lost
my sight, I could see. I drew
a calligraphy of letters,
a Braille of seeing.

These lines are
not visible. Read
them to me now.

©Brenda Clews 2006

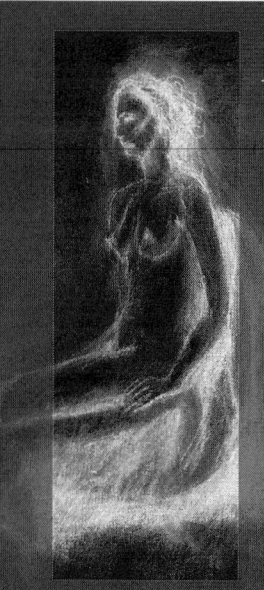

➤ Scrawls

When he couldn't speak, he wrote. What did he say? I've forgotten.

The sheets are in the blue zipper folder, lined paper with scrawls in blue felt pen, in my filing cabinet crammed in the storage unit. All the cards of condolences are there too. Without his glasses, he couldn't see what he was writing. Notes to his daughter. She kept them, blue felt lines like a bodice over a constricted rib cage.

➤ Lip Read

The silencers.

I learnt to lip read.

You read me in my absence. You occur in my language of sight.

~ *Writings of 'Who'*

I seek who allows me to write. In the sunlit corridor, perhaps. An encounter with my eclipsed twin, who answers through this writing. Who is the narrator conversing with me in these words that I relay to you as we converse? Who haunts us from within?

Who is writing?

Surely not our speaking voice.

Poetry evokes us, like the gradual lightness of dawn. If the trope of light didn't burn, corrode our vision, that is. Sometimes I want to keep my secrets secret.

Down the dark corridors of time, our shadows cast into the future. Where the doors open, and close, and open, the spurious wind blowing through. Shutters cannot stay shut. We are haunted by ourselves, ghosts moving through ourselves.

Can we have thoughtless words?* A discourse bereaved of its cry?

Spurious, "At the end of my strength," Sep 26, 2006, http://spurious.typepad.com/spurious/2006/09/at_the_end_of_m.html

◝ *Inflamed*

An inflamed belly—was it the prunes, dried apricots, dark chocolate discs, Guinness draft, muesli and raw sugar fermenting until I became ill—the late hour, I clicked on the wrong tab, it disappeared. Poems cannot be rewritten. Will what surfaced from the currents of words reappear? Or, like a melted iceberg, gone, become ocean.

Only the title remains, "How Are We To Face Each Other?" Out into the day, I ache, light-headed, still swimming in the depths of the emotional disaster last week, the emailing, the words, the decisions, the silences, the loss.

Incomprehensible on the edge of.

Aren't they all edges?

And where is.

~ *Letter in Saffron*

I write in the corner of a Parsee restaurant that drew me, after city blocks of walking, with a warmth of its Indian colours and curtained light.

Under my plate, an orange flower radiates out from white stitching on the tablecloth under the clear plastic. It matches the saffron rice. I pour a delicate gold stream of olive oil over my salad, then lime juice. A kebab, sour cream, rice, a stewed tomato before me, I toast you, *mon Monsieur*, with mellow wine, and watch the babies of two Indian couples.

They sit in high chairs. They form rudimentary wordsounds, "blaah, ma-ma-ma" with joyful loud. Their mothers in sweatsuits "shhh," and point.

Wide brown eyes gaze at me.

The men, starch white shirts, dark business suits, ignore everyone and talk only to each other.

Is marriage a turbulent stone to hold while she thrashes in the water, *Monsieur*, trying to keep energies contained?

The Parsee woman at work told me about her wedding dress of white lace and how afterwards, she would wear a honey mustard sari with gold threads sewn through it.

Saffron, everywhere, *Monsieur*.

This letter is composed of strands of saffron.

∼ Remember the Night ...

When, you,
without closure, engulfed me?

When I disappeared into your vastness,
became lost in you, lost 'I'?

Everywhere you touched, mountains,
valleys, plains, the ocean in me,
parted, shook, opened.

Do you remember how we,
two sighs enfolded in each other?

Breath of love. I speak of romance tonight;
forgive me, *Monsieur.* Afterwards,
we did not speak of it.

On the surface of the water that resists
before you fall in, that edge of sweetness.

Mon amour, now it is like sitting in a darkened room
with a screen of scenes before us, our hands close,
but not touching.

You are so far away.

∼ Grammars

Monsieur, you are an invisible character, a reference outside the writing for whom the writing is written; your eyes read as the reader reads. You were conceived as a literary device; then, I discovered we knew each other intimately.

We meet at the edge of the text.
These words unfold
through the syntax of your absent presence
in the writing.

∼ Exile

Those of whom I speak, *Monsieur*, are embedded in grammars too. As syntaxes and lexicons of unique verbal patterns, we are bound by a grammar which shapes our relationships.

The man who teaches pedagogy says, "What we must never do:

• Patronize, reduce, laud, ridicule, dismay
• Simplify, bowdlerize, censure, censor
• Wield discourse as spectacle
• Wield discourse as power
• Wield discourse contemptuously"*

Or silence each other.

We humiliate those we exile. By ignoring them, we remove their voice.

If we refuse to listen, they cannot speak.
If they speak they will not be heard.
We have created a hole in the grammar of our connection
which divests the speaker we did not want to listen to
of a speaking voice that is heard.

---

* blah-feme, "fragments of a manifesto for a radical pedagogy," Sep 19, 2006
http://blahfeme.typepad.com/blahfeme/2006/09/fragment_of_a_m.html

Monsieur: it happened to me. My enunciations formed an uncomfortable anomaly in the grammar of the group. Without an anxiety about the rigours of practice, I was not struggling in the way I was meant to. Given the reputation of the group, I could not be overtly ridiculed; instead, I was ignored. An absent presence. Silence was wielded by those who formed an inner circle, carefully, so my diminishing welcome would not be evident to the others. What happened *Monsieur*? Exile.

~ *aphatos, speechless, not speakable*

Speechless,
we speak.

The making
mute.

If we don't hear each other,
how can we listen?

~ *Potestas, Power*

Where I was cast off.

Power, the ability to do.
Power, having others believe.

We watch ourselves
with internalized surveillance.

How are we shaped by that which we wish to be accepted by?

∿ *Spectre*

She walks the sea wall. A parade of black, coats, pants, dresses, and flashes of red, the ribbon and feather in her black felt fedora. Her white face, the black hair and lurid red lipstick, a spectre.

When she gazes at us
beating warmth of our blood
we cannot escape,
our unblinking eyes

> *The straining eye always resembles an eye of the blind, sometimes the eye of the dead, at that precise moment when mourning begins: it is still open, a pious hand should soon come to close it; it would recall a portrait of the dying.**

The woman in black trailing the sea wall, her hair, its tendrils and curls coiling in the salt spray, turns us to marble, pale green veins in the rock. She splatters us with red the colour of her fingernail polish.

The Gorgon creates a stage of unmoving characters, her silent companions.

She laughs at my drained creativity; I know this woman. The blood drains from my lips: I am silenced.

I, mute.

Unspeaking.

∿ *Stony Glance*

The seawall, my inner lashing waves. Salt tears.

Her parrot, cinnabar and virid feathers, mocks, repeating endlessly the soulless words that echo on the sea spray while she laughs.

---

*Jacques Derrida, *Memoirs of the Blind: The Self-Portrait and Other Ruins*, trans. Pascale-Anne Brault and Michael Naas (Chicago: The University of Chicago Press, 1993), p. 57.
Why is there cruelty? Don't ask.

It is; we are.

I want to be a tidal wave
but I withdraw.

Describe the figure of jealousy, of derision?

Is jealousy the overweening desire to upstage the other?

To cast them away,
stones of silence?

I evade her stony glance
with *questions*.

❧ Polishing the Rocks

Barrage of surf.

Fear holds me
captive; like the Eight of Swords,* bound and blind-folded, unseeing and
scared, though all the swords are stuck, blade-first, in the ground.

It's not a question of safety, *Monsieur*. It's a lifelong problem with creativity
that I have, *she has*. *Monsieur*, I split myself into a third person, a *she*. That is
me. Or *her*.

Does it matter who swirls in the salt spray, its turbulences of disappearing
foam?

Is the invisible rendered visible
through our perceptions?

I am the subject. I cannot look upon myself lest I turn into bloodless
reflection. In the mirror, the Medusa.

An unblinking gaze. The object of the subject is the subject. Only in the self-
portrait does the ruin of the self break down. We are decomposing into text.

Into iconography.

Immortal.

Immortalizing ourselves in time: statues, broken rubble of stones amid the
hissing of the broiling waves.

---

*Eight of Swords in the Rider-Waite Tarot deck.

~ *The Medusa*

Can you know
the depths of the anguish, *Monsieur*?
Deep in the grammar of the self
where it unravels
defies coherency,
laws of linguistic construction.
Being forced
to look
with unblinking eyes.

Terror of catatonia,
this self-portrait.

A work is at once order
and its ruin. And
these weep for one
another.*

My head unwraps
in the mirror
like a ribbon,
or writhing
snake.

This writing:
is it risk-taking?
Am I subverting myself?

—In this emotional storm
of words—

Apollo, rising full of pride, held out the
head of the Medusa to this grotesquely
uncouth Dionysian power.**

"Nietzsche sees the
Medusa between them,
like a figure of death," says
Derrida.***

She who turns life into art
with her gaze.
Flesh become stone,
pigment, pixel, celluloid.

The immortalizer

who
kills us?

I weep on an altar
of rainbow
serpents, on
shed skin.

The coils
in my jewel-studded hair
cut, a mass of
deathly
serpent
eyes.

---

*Jacques Derrida, *Memoirs of the Blind: The Self-Portrait and Other Ruins*, trans. Pascale-Anne Brault and Michael Naas (Chicago: The University of Chicago Press, 1993), p. 122.
**Friedrich Nietzsche, *The Birth of Tragedy*, trans. Walter Kaufman (New York: Vintage Books, 1967), p. 39, as quoted in Derrida, p. 123.
***Derrida, p. 122.

ᵔᵕ *On the Beach*

Polished pebbles, smooth glass baubles, tangles of fishing wire, water-logged boots, seaweed, translucent shells, chipped, molluscs and sea urchins, dead, cadaverous detritus, swollen along the glimmering band of sand.

I see her on sea walks. In a long black skirt, she gazes out to sea, grief on her slightly wetted face from the spray of the water on the rocks that she stands on, and something indefinable, lit from within, but subtle, like sunset spilling out of her eyes.

The coast is empty.

I am not sure who I am.

Me, her, or you, or a transfigured god,
a Medusa-lady, the curls in my hair tightly coiled in the salt spray,
an image-maker.

Blue dancers leap and fall, disappearing bubbles of sea foam.

You are the edge of the waves that tip over. When the peak cannot hold itself aloft and falls like a dancer letting go of taut tension and plunging. Or perhaps it is words that fall into froth.

We are standing on the shore of oceans that encase the earth.

Let me bathe in your words, salt rinsing raw passion and let our vision be as infinite as the skyline.

Am I in love with you, and who?

My unbidden,
holy muse.

∾ Leaving Time

Time "... is something we are constantly involved in creating.
Like a work of art."*

A few days ago, mid-evening, a moment in my meditation where I disappeared. When I came back, I knew I had been gone: vacuous, no thought or memory. It wasn't a moment of sleep. Was it an experience of obliteration... of no self, no individuality?

"Everything I am was gone for those few minutes. Even the consciousness that tracks experience was absent.

*"As I re-entered my life, I realized I'd been nowhere."**

Saying this created dissension. An insistence on stupor, that it's common, that it's not Satori. Where do such labels come from? I, who belong to no 'system.' Who am not interested in the project of enlightenment. Does it threaten when someone escapes time?

Ultimately, then: mystery. Insanity, or Love.

---

* Peter Hoeg, *Borderliners*, trans. Barbara Haveland (New York: Farrar, Straus and Giroux, 1994), p. 236-7.
**Journal entry, February 2006.

~ Tidal Patterns

Once, the tide remained high. Without clams or seaweed, the *Tsimshian**
went hungry. Raven knew what lay under the blue glistening robes of water.

When he wrapped his blanket of black feathers around his strong shoulders,
he flew. His sharp eyes watched, looking. Scanning the edges of the ocean,
he found her.

Tightly she held the tide-line in her hands. She would not release the ocean
to rhythmically rise and fall on the beach, or draw back from it, leaving
washed treasures, clams, seaweed, shells and shiny pebbles.

Why did the old woman hold the tide-line so tightly in her lined, papery
hands? Lodged in her small house on the edge of the sea, she gripped the
waters in the lifelines on her palms. Who can tell from the mass of mounds
and lines on her hands how she bid the edges of the great water be still?

Inside her sun-bleached house with closed eyes, she imagined the ocean or
saw it with visionary sight. She sat, the tide-line, her hands, the one
interconnected with the other, like a fisherman's net, weeping tears of salt.

Raven dropped from the sky, a shadow of black feathers. He sat beside her
and groaned, holding his belly, saying he had eaten too many clams. He
broke her meditation, and she stood and went to look at the clams, but he
pushed her and she fell. Then he poured sand in her eyes so that she was
blinded. Pulling the tide-line out of her hands, tearing the lifeline from her,
he released the hold on the waters and the tide at last fell.

Crazy old woman on the edge of the ocean of time, time's burden, that
weight of life-giving water.

And so the ocean drew back its mantle of blue robes and the people feasted.

There were bonfires on the beaches and a festival of clambakes that lasted
days until everyone's bellies were swollen with food.

Who was the blind old woman crying on the beach with the torn hands?

Raven in raucous joviality passing from one feasting party to the next found himself before the old woman, who spoke, "Raven, heal my eyes so I may see again." Raven, trickster-figure, Promethean fire-stealer, knew the Gods must be bargained with, appeased. He struck a deal: "Old woman of the sea, I will heal you, but you must promise to let the tide-line go twice a day so that the people may gather food from the beaches." The old woman agreed and so he rinsed the sand out of her eyes. Thus Raven ensured the lifelines of the people, their continuity.

As I walk the desolate beach strewn with empty clam shells, seaweed, the detritus of modern civilization, I want to find her, and find out why, the withholding.

I want to know why she denounces me, if she does, or those like her.

And take the caul she has wrapped me in off: to breathe, to see.

I spin like Tiresias under an unrelenting sun.
Why are black feathers strewn in my hair?
My eyes, gritty and sore, are on fire
I see only flaring volcanoes
A red rage of light;
On this windless day
How did my eyes fill with sand?
My hands bleed as I write.
For what do I weep?

---

*Tsimshian story first read in *Keepers of the Earth* by Michael J. Caduto and Joseph Bruchac (Fulcrum Publishing, 1988): https://books.google.ca/books?id=HsK1IPPUAl8C&pg=PA103&lpg=PA103&dq#v

❧ *Death of Time*

My words silt in the paddies of time, flooded with being.

Time drowns us.

Break out of time: escapee.
Leave the encircling fields of the centuries.

Plummet silence.

Breathe without tracking, calibration, rates, or seizures.

❧ Pythia, Priestess of Apollo

Step onto a floor of hissing snakes, locked for the night in an underground cavern. If you move, they will strike, venom filling your veins. Remain mute and immobile as a statue through the vigil for the priestesses to find you alive in the morning.

The fumes of the python enable us to foresee.

Allow the snakes to slither over your warm body, for it is damp and chilly in the black caves and they are cold-blooded, without response, fear, shaking, or terror. Remain rigid and you will be safe, though you will never see the world the same way again. You will survive if you know how.

You cannot sleep; you may not awaken. If they bite, your blood, enraged with poison, your throat, swollen shut to air. The venom paralyzes — you may scream but, like being entombed in stone sarcophagi, no sound emerges: catatonia. If a tiny, young snake jabs your skin with its sharp tooth and releases venom from its sac into your bloodstream, you may live; if it is a large, older snake, you will not.

You hallucinate them; the stone walls of the tunnelled lairs are empty, white.

You hear gliding; they have been starved for this night. In the darkness, they smell you. They coil around your ankles and wrists, waist and neck, across your forehead. They wrap themselves around you, savouring your warmth.

Medusa has come and gone,
her hair of hissing.

Like a landlady at the *Omphalos*
with a secret initiation of the adept in her basement.

They sit on a tripod over the venomous vapour, answering questions, all having survived a night in the depths of the snake caves, the Oracles at Delphi.

~ *Ouroboros*

Monsieur, your absence, I thought you had forgotten me. A spelunker of snakes? It alarms you, this imagination of mine.

I hallucinate snakes.

They slither down my back from the showerhead, small pythons, black mambas, in stone grey or black. I become rigid with fear, the hot hissing water.

I ground myself: concentrate on the tiles, the shower curtain, the soap, the washcloth. Push sensations of snakes dropping on my head, slithering down my back, out. Remnants of memories of watching the poor creatures swinging on sticks in the air until their backbones broke and they went limp. It was a game, in a circle laughing.

Terrors of a memory gone awry, misplacing splices of the past out-of-context in the present: I step onto floors thick with writhing serpents, but they aren't real. This phobia of mine.

Freud's sexual interpretation, too narrow; Jung's better, except that they don't automatically signify psychic fragmentation if they're not dynamically balanced, as revealed in spontaneously individuated mandalas, symbols of wholeness.

I studied serpents and the winged kind, dragons, in Western art, explored the mythologies. From Egyptian cobra worship, to Greco-Roman Medusas, to the Judaeo-Christian myth of the Fall from Eden due to the guiles of the Satanic snake, to all the St. Georges' and other Courtly Love heroes fighting all the dragons who had taken over the land and were demanding fresh virgins, to modern day snake cults and Goddess lore, to the R-Complex, or brain at the base of our skulls, the reptilian one, that controls automatic functions.

For me, *Monsieur*: the power of the Minoan Snake Goddess who holds live serpents in each hand, and the Greek understanding that serpents enable us to enter the mysteries of the chthonic earth itself: a motile symbol of creativity.

I collect serpent jewellery. Wrapped around my fingers are silver snake rings, silver serpents coil around the tubes that form my dangling earrings, another embraces a crystal pendant that hangs on a chain and falls between my breasts, and my arms are braceleted by silver cobras.

Once when I was young, in a bikini sunbathing alone, a man, himself no more than a messenger, a hallucination, approached, wearing khaki clothes and snake boots, as if out of the African jungle, in his hand a choke of snakes that he held over my body, and said, threatening to drop them on me, "Will you write?"

My muse is a Lady of Serpents.

She is the Kundalini, the lightning that travels from chakra to chakra in the awakening.

Yes, I have painted snakes, but they don't belong on canvas; rather, they are the artist's brushes themselves.

Monsieur, I have always known that *what terrifies me is my source.*

∾ *Evanescence*

It is fleeting, ephemeral, fragile — beauty,

life.

Silence of the deep sleep, death,

of non-being,

eternity,

the norm.

➳ *Reading Writing Letters*

When the letters began curling like tiny writhing black snakes on the page,

I lost

the ability to read.

Letters floated between the paper and my eyes, hovered, hallucinatory, unreadable, and I couldn't catch them or make them form words or sentences though I knew coherency was there, below the

writhing floating

if I could just
make them sit

still.

When it came back, focus, and the words stayed on the page,

I gluttonized on words, gorged.

I pushed myself through tomes; I let books open other books;
I kept copious notes in ledgers, dozens of journals.

I read all night. I read with urgency, as if my life depended on it. Did I waste my youth reading Plato and Aristotle, Augustine and Aquinas, Bacon and Shakespeare?

It's all fleeting.

But when the words stayed still, lying in neat rows on the pages, I raced through them. Who knew how long I had?

～ *interlacings of love*

I can feel your presence, *mon amour*, pressing in on me and I imagine you vividly in this room whose walls are covered in paintings, and can almost see you in the night light, as if you are present and flowing around me, but you are not here and yet I know you are, like a spectre, because you love me.

It is an odd thing, *Monsieur*, that I feel loved by those who have abandoned me.

And of course, I love

you

too.

∾ Masks

The women wear masks, watching each other. They move stealthily between the men who are gazing on the objects of their desire, not grasping the emotional complexity of the game stalking them.

She will drop remarks in his ear, scathing, denigrating ones, innuendos, attempt to cause aversion in him towards the targeted woman, and she will succeed. Her insidious voice hardens the heart, propels what negates. She conquers her competition by derision, causing the other to disappear.

What if her mask is peeled off, her words exposed?

Who will be safe?

∾ Lustre

Fend and defend—do not puncture yourself from within, no shame, or self-blame.

Shield yourself from jealousy's spikes. Don't yield or drift, trying to be less than you are.

Be careful but bold, and give everything, don't withhold. It's a social maze. Know who is your friend and who your enemy. Be attuned. Be brave.

Blaze with radiance.

~ *Dance of the Sarong*

Wrapping raw silk around my shoulders, torso, breasts, head and arms, I am trapped. I dance like a slave seeking a freedom that is terrifying. With nothing to constrain you, fetter, contain, weigh, what would you do, who would you be?

If we could ignore being watched, read, observed, judged, about the unceasing gaze of the other, what would we be, produce, live?

In what ways do we keep each other in check, clipped, chained, trapped?

I push elbows against the tight fabric and turn and fall and gyrate in a self-imposed prison. In shades of blue, the sarong echoes the burqa, dress code of societies which contain the energy of women in well-defined boundaries. Images shape my dance, ancient Egyptian mummies, torture victims, Michelangelo's slaves, enslavements from without and when we enslave ourselves. I dance a life's struggles.

Twirling, fighting for release along the wall, private anguish is visible. I am enrapt with an invisibility that gives me the freedom to struggle for inner freedom.

When the dance is over, I peel off the sarong like a ribbon of skin and sit in the circle of women, wondering if any of us is closer to who we are.

∼ *Approach*

The configuration of your desire, *Monsieur*, is complex. The beauty of women, how does it move you?

Scent of her kisses, tender cleavage, your lips, the way she holds you in her tiny hands, what it would be like to plunge yourself into her. She in whom you would obliterate.

Lust and bliss, loin and heart a daze. Or perhaps it is frenzy, a blindness?

Do we fall into what dissembles us?
A whirlpool, its swirling torpor,
undressing us,
naked against the onrush.

Are we always approaching what we can never give ourselves to?

∼ *Strengthen*

Instead of fleeing into fissures
withdrawing into a shell
masking with silence
remaining while rushing away
the wave rose high
surging in sunlight
milky green underside
proud, and
defended.

∼ *Sighting*

On the beach they throw rocks, sharp shell bits and driftwood at the strange
fish flopping out of the water; then they stop, acknowledge, back off.

Having met the fear of difference, two obverse cultures reckon with each
other. One half-submerged, gasping water and air; the other, only air-sucking.

On the shore, waves tore the air.

No-one was hurt; the shouting group withdrew from the edge.

The flopping into the coiling wave as it drew back.

A miracle; they called it a miracle sighting,
that day.

~> Stare

Eyes that stare. Impassive, in the rocking cars of the underground trains, brown or blue, tiny, beady, at young women. Seated, watching. Unwavering, bleak.

Her glistening, manicured curls, gym-toned lithe body, tight jeans or skirts, tiny butt-geared jackets, dusted with golden glow.

Energetic, ambitious, sweet. Cadences of voices on phones when the cars break out of the earth and glide on metal tracks under the vast sky.

Old, heavy, arthritic, hair like grey wire. If such fixed, harsh eyes could suck beauty in. Beauty would be siphoned out of that diaphanous thing sitting so lightly on the seat, oblivious. But events will mark her too, face of powdered crevices, make-up collecting in the networks of wrinkles, the soft sagging skin.

To place mirrors before those who watch: see your reality, you who are no longer. Why do the generations do this to each other? Cold, impassive, unsmiling stare.

Jealousy.

Bitterness, its terrible face.

Undo it! Take off the mask! Ma Mer! I beseech!

～ Glare

How do we detect the dark motive?

～ Chains

She stalks the seawall, stopping, staring at the unmoving horizon. Perhaps she is waiting, remembering. Her furious, angry eyes, forlorn. Was her heart broken, and then re-broken before it mended?

Her arms of black lace, black brocade skirt, she dresses as if from another century, the red silk scarf at her neck like a flag of conquest, of the surrendered, broken heart.

She paces; stops.

Sometimes she screeches. Gulls land on her shoulders. Sand flies in her dyed vine-black wind-streamed hair. Earrings the colour of ripe cherries dangle from her earlobes. Spray wets her tear-swollen face.

If you talk to her, she will stare blankly, or scream at you.

Attack, belittle, accuse.

Let her pace. The white cuffs of waves chain enough.

∾ *Unpossessed*

I have no reason not to believe you, *Monsieur*. You, who are cosmopolitan, a superb lover.

Fresh oranges in the Aegean Sea;
Hot Springs in Banff; or Ikaria, Greece;
Paris for art, or New York,
and women.

Monsieur, we could explore the *erotique*, except you are not here. Words dance in the air across the spaces of tables, phones, pages or screens. The ceaseless flow of loving words caressing, licking me with tongues of fire, yet without touching. Sometimes you prefer the intimacy of distance.

You are far away, listening.

Nobody *can have me*; I cannot *have* anybody. It is a reality, *mon amour*.

∾ *Amour Doux*

Consciousness dissembles, *Monsieur*. Where I lay flew apart while composing itself.

Monsieur! I would never speak in riddles. Stop laughing. Why do you call me delightfully irreverent? Besides, I don't mean in any absolute or invisible ways; nor as semiotic symbol. The 'noumenon of the phenomenon'? Sort of, yes ... as long as they're both the same, that is.

The forms of the world are like a waterfall that constantly changes yet maintains its pattern. Does that help?

You're making me laugh, *mon amour*. What do you mean, Niagara Falls is eroding into disappearance? *Sweet love*, perhaps that's it.

I floated stably in the tenuousness of the deeper permanence of existence, an existence that will fragment and float away.

Changes rise through the layers of my life. No, *Monsieur*, oh *vous charmez*, I am not referring to sheets! I slept and when I woke, it was as if the continents of my life were floating. Where was the ground?

Flux? Oh, you make me giggle, Heraclitean, sure. Or Relativistic time and space that is itself fluxes of events that unfold, close, open, shift, metamorphose, glide, disperse, flow and hold still.

Energy is the ecstasy of form. Do you not agree?

Yes, *amour doux*, I do remember those enfolded nights of ecstasies.

Yes, I was alone. Why do you, who are so far away, care? I woke into heat with the goldenness of the sun all around, only it was night, the softness of vellum cotton sheets. I always think of you! Why do you ask? In the world that is a series of intersecting, coalescing systems, nothing can be gained or lost. No, not like the stock market; *Monsieur*, you are silly tonight!

It's the momentum of things, forever oscillating.

The Ground of Being, *mon amour*, is no ground at all.

～ *Clarity*

Loud rapping at the top of a small escalator, on the old, mottled stone floor. Transit riders, hearing the commotion, turn to another series of stairs. It is dark up there. I am tired, climb up.

She is at the top, agitated.

Black wool coat, skin pale as glazed porcelain, hair so black light disappears into it, mid-length, curly. Eyes half-closed, a bluish light. She smacks the white-tipped cane hard, like a weapon, this baton-feeler of the terrain of the ground of the subway tunnels. "Where's the exit? Why won't anyone help me? Where's the ticket-taker?" She hit the cane perilously close to the top of the escalator when I guide her away.

"What are you looking for? A train?"

"No! I want to get out of here! Why won't anyone help me?!"

She is on the wrong floor. She becomes more flustered when she discovers she was given wrong directions. I guide her to the elevator, press the button. When the door opens I guide her in, press the button for the upper floor. All the while I tell her what we are doing. I ask no questions of her. After we ascend and the doors open, I take her to the exit, and, holding her shoulders, point her to the way out. I worry about her vulnerability, and wish I had time to ensure she gets wherever she is going.

My bus arrives 5 minutes later and as we pull out of the station I see her, having only gone 500 yards on the sidewalk, hair flying wildly with her flapping coat in the high wind, tapping the sidewalk with staccato jabs, finding her way despite.

That she cannot see
is clear.

～ Gaze

Yesterday,
the bus stop,
all the people's heads
turned, watching.

Gaze of anxiety.

The blind woman tapping
her way forward.

～ Desire

Can I see myself as you see me?

The gaze is whose gaze? And what is desire, *Monsieur*?

Desire is more than fantasy; it is a will towards, a propulsion. Desire materializes us.

Eros flows differently now, the topography's changed, or the flow of the meridians irrigates differently.

Desire materializes us only to
dematerialize us.
It's a paradox, *mon amour.*

I incarnate deeply in my erogenous body
as I disperse under your touch, turn molten.
Until we are nothing
but pulsing
filaments
lit by each other's passion.

But I imagine this, *Monsieur.*

In the space of desire
where my fantasies enact.

∾ All-Seeing

When he stood, in the peace of post-coital stillness, and said, 'I want to destroy you,' she waged a battle for her life for the next 15 years.

No-one emerged unscathed.

She rose, a soot-blackened woman, from the fine layers of silted taupe ashes, with scorched feet, able to see in all directions.

∾ Coiled

In the vision behind her vision, a helmet of hair, tightly coiled serpents. Alive, the colour of alabaster. Why are they tightly coiled around her statuesque head? Do they grow from her scalp or do they merely cling to her head? What do they eat? Realism is not the point of myth.

I hear hissing. My muse is calling.

Do aesthetics of art and finance arise from the same roots?

What does the Gorgon want?

Writhing, coiling in these numbered halls
papered with endless account statements.

∿ *Waves of Words*

Words float under my rib cage, cascade over my heart, and waterfall down my body. Invisible, but you knew. I could see you reading me.

Like a streak of fish, a discourse of signifiers referring to each other, signifiers whose identities are only their relations to other signifiers, an entire system mediating reality.

The colour; the ocean.

Floating like thought.

But, then.

The discourse into which we are born is a discourse of love, at the depths. Never mind the story.

Love creates itself.

What else do we need?

∼ *Absence*

Monsieur, you exist in your absence.
Not only that,
but you exist in my absence.

The nexus of you
renders love possible.

Which carries on without either of us.

∼ *Esoteric*

the inner meaning of us, our relation,
cannot be grasped or apprehended in this language
or any other language
of the heart

even as it structures our desire

∼ *Intimacy*

Waves of words flow over the world: in the absence of the objects to which they refer; in the absence of the author who set them in their sequences on their journeys.

Phrases, sentences, paragraphs, flowing on. Picked up and read, retained momentarily. Onward, joining, dispersing, shoals of words, tides of words, flowing through our consciousnesses, into our ears, our eyes, and out of our lips, from our fingertips.

The weave of words that weaves our world, shaping it into familiar patterns, without which it would all fall apart and yet which like a membrane separates us from reality. Mimicry. Artistry. Telling us how to see, how to be. The language that shapes us, shaping. Weave of words sculpting.

Is inseparable from time which structures us, organizes us into communal cohesion.

Who cares if we are carriers of the word, transmitters of culture?

The intimacy of love sighing, your lips

kissing you, I
melt in your mouth

⮑ *Money*

The earth turns on its axis but the world turns on money. Capital sloshes through the global markets with the force of daily oceanic tides.

⮑ *Molten*

The sky molten, *mon amour.* A broil of clouds in my heart. How long can I wait?

The silence in which I wait.

You cannot know, *mon homme chéri.*

I do not wish to burden you.

A relational line, a trajectory, a specific set of connections, patterns, motions into. Fire of desire. The threads extinguish themselves in the smouldering flame. What is moving towards erases itself as it burns, charred, blown away in the wind.

Will you catch me?

Or will you let me pass by?

~ *Sea-Break*

The sea wall, broached. The tide swells. Water flies in howling wind, undoes the brick, mortar and concrete. The barrier is lost.

There is nothing to keep her from sweeping out to sea, her black dress like a wave of crows flying about her.

Her eyes are lit with terror as the water rises, foaming.

She shrieks at the turbulent sky, her voice joins the screaming winds.

She stands on an outcrop. The water swirls around her feet, but doesn't wash her away. The rock holds her safe.

Her face is a venom of fury
when she sees me.

What does she desire?

∾ *Fear*

Monsieur,

It is the ancient fear of entrapment.

∾ *Capture*

When you are lovingly diffident, sweet but often absent, I am comfortable; yet I need your ardour.

If you appear to discard me, for you never do, I can breathe; if you cling, I panic, sending invisible arrows to scare you off, so you will shy away. Mixed messages, subliminal, not knowingly. I'd like to stop, if only I knew how.

For me to be still, and not consider fleeing, and be your woman is difficult, even if I am your woman.

Capture terrifies me.

Like conventional relationships.

Approaching but never arriving. Hidden in each other's lives. Intimacy, this dance of closeness. Which can't settle.

Can we roam through each other's hearts
like oceanic tides?

~ *Tempest*

She crawled along the key. She chose not to give in.

When the winds subsided, they brought her back. They stabilized her with intravenous fluids, medication. They checked her blood, ran a CAT scan, an MRI. In her stupor, she relented.

I could feel the tension of resistance dissipate like a boxing glove gone limp. The stuffing disappeared. She could no longer hit; the psychic force of her anger gone.

Her black dress lay on the floor, salty and ragged. At the roots of her dull black hair, a blanched white tide rising. She looked old and strangely newborn in her hospital green gown. Unlike herself.

Only her fingernails, glaring red.

Would it build again, the tempest?

Perhaps.

~ *Fever*

Was it that she'd always had a raging fever?

Does rage have a temperature, and had it now peaked, and was broken?

∼ Weight

The weight of words, *Monsieur,*

refer to what is almost out of reach. Emotion, idea, situation, description, approximating, never fully expressing what they create and shape. We are not feral. Culture moves through us, syncopates its rhythms in us, punctuates us.

veils of words and images drifting over the world

∼ Hallucination

Within the film of my life, creating the story I live.

It shapes outer events. The world coheres to my version.

Do you understand that
the world
is a mass hallucination?

That we have agreed
to hallucinate
and we teach our children.

~ *Wilderness*

"I don't find anything out there. I find my own relation to the spaces. We see nature with our cultivated eyes. Again, there is no true nature, there is only your and my construct." Olufur Eliason.*

You say the wilderness you walk in every day exists.

You have named every tree, shrub, bird, insect. You move through a wilderness of labels, of theories of ecosystems, of words and images that describe it. You cohere this experience of wilderness; without you, it wouldn't exist.

How can we see but through our own perceptions? A trained and honed perceptual apparatus with its own categories, ethic and aesthetic.

Could we stumble through the bush blindly — what would we see?

What of the feral child's experience of the wilderness —
raised by wolves, who move by scent
on all fours, tear at the beating
body of fur and blood with bared teeth?

Only the subjective, the relational. There is no objective universe.

We create the world we live in.

---

*Olufur Eliason: http://www.olafureliasson.net/index.html

∾ light glancing

The waves I watch from the window,
imagining across the dreamscape.

Dream the world.

"... That summer all the world
was soul and water, light glancing off peaks."
Michael Sims*

---

*Michael Sims, "The Summer You Learned to Swim," from The Happiness of Animals
(Monkey Sea Editions): http://writersalmanac.publicradio.org/index.php?date=2006/11/24

∾ Constructions

The original substratum, nature, the wilderness,
constructed. Like that burning ball in the sky
that is not sun, light, right, might, *sol invictus*, or illumina,
that remains unknown.

Can I burn under the artificial sun
in the simulated weather of
the Turbine Hall of the Tate Museum in London?
Will the fog
of the weather project
hide me?

⌇ Wild Man

Monsieur, you are staid, professional, quiet, muted.

When you strip your clothes, the frenzy begins. How can such passion hide under a veneer smooth as the pinstripes of a suit?

An erotic energy
smouldering bush fire.

~ *Mist*

Dense fog today. The world is impenetrable. Only the whiteness of cloud. Breathe the cool moisture; walk blindly forward. The ground remains; the route is the same. Follow your feet. According to the Hopi, there are two kinds of time, the unmanifest and the manifest. We are between. The world that is coming to be in its ecstasy is not yet born. The fog carries us through. Float on the breath of the mist.

~ *Tide-Line*

They disappear. They always return. The men who love me. It is too early to say if it is a pattern.

Sometimes I feel like the woman in the sea cottage who holds the tide-line tight in her hands. Then I don't drift in and out like the moon-pulled sea; then I remain, present.

~ *Disguise*

Sometimes we have to pretend to be who we are to be who we are.

If I disguise you in metaphors, it is to reveal you. Or myself. Or the inter-connections that interweave us.

∾ Lies

Today, like a mistress of Pythonus, envy wore black hair and a blazer with a red chiffon blouse and a smiling demeanour in the office tower that could be anywhere in the world.

∾ Fog Lights

Through the fog, forms. Other buildings, sky. In the corneas of my eyes.

The corona of the sun, hidden.

There are no sunspots today, no solar flares, no solar storms.

The world is quiet. Lying under a blanket of mist. The wind is absent. Birds fly blindly.

Do you have your fog lights on as you make your way along the snaking highways? Somebody stops or swerves in the flow of cars and there is a pile-up. Buckled metal and torn and broken lives, but not yours. You are caught in the traffic and are late.

Not to meet me, but the others.

I am behind the fog.

➷ River of Light

From high in the corporate tower, in the distance drifting fog, the curving highway, everybody driving home, a flowing river of light.

White bloodstream of the city.

➷ The Lake

The lake rushes, potencies of green, grey and blue. It reflects. Mist drifts in soft streams with pale blue patchily appearing and sun that reveals its presence on the blinding whiteness of cumulus clouds. The sky is a steamer rushing by.

In the east, the mist is broiling in a squall and the water froths with whitecaps and it looks as if the turbulent sky has fallen into the water.

Patches of snake green appear and disappear on the surface of the water according to the whims of the fleeting sky.

The winds blow the mist at velocities I can only imagine. What appears like steam billows past the window at racing speeds.

Despite the rippling surging rhythms of the lake, the harbours in the islands are moments of meditation.

∼ The View from the Lake

Letters and numbers, words and money, invisible, flowing, continuous traffic on the highways splayed in all directions, transferring, shaping, corroding landscapes.

From the Island View Room, its antiques and Persian carpet high in the corporate bank tower, the sky is an opaque pale grey. The rain has stopped; it is thickly overcast.

In the distance the Scarborough Bluffs are lit by sun.

White walls of a white city of vision.

∼ Driving

When we drove he kept his hand high on my inner thigh. Did I like it? Of course I did, *Monsieur.*

∼ Liqueur du Feu

Driving me home, you softly asked, 'I'd like to lie naked next to you,' and I thought how warm and comforting. Only when our clothes lay on the ground you became fire and I melted into liqueur, hot sweetness all over you.

～ Rigid

Did anything change?

I don't think so.

Once she was back in her unkempt house, where she was looked after until she regained her strength, the tirades began again. She said she was living out of a dumpster which was ludicrous. She lashed out at anyone who was younger, brighter, more beautiful. Which was most of the women in the world since she was old and on the decline.

The black habits continued. Dark and flapping with a cane at the seashore, a nun-like crone. Except for the florid red lipstick, the crimson suede gloves, the cherry red French lace petticoat under the thick layers of black burlap when the wind blew.

～ Masque du Shaman

Dreaming, *Monsieur*, I saw your face like a carnival masque of clouds floating, and emptiness, the void itself, where your eyes and open mouth are.

A burqa of white around my head, the snowy landscape. The purity of the whole unbroken light, its whiteness.

～ Roar of the Tidal Pattern

She left too many spaces between her paragraphs,

and they encroached.

∽ Spaces

So many white spaces
between paragraphs.

A white font? Whitecaps of
hidden writing...

She talks under her breath, muttering, blaming; I hear her the way one hears
the ocean in a seashell held up to one's ear.

In those spaces between the blocks of black words.

Virid and cinnabar feathers lying about, the swishing of endless sea foam
beneath her squawking, the way she belittles us.

∽ Shooting Star

A moment of confidence that's gone.

～ Trail

The trail, *Monsieur*, is a decoy. It does not reveal my whereabouts, or my perspective. I could be elsewhere in the terrain where it is dense, dark and dangerous. You would never guess from my notes and messages. I could be escaping our field of connections, and yet appear to be available, even stable. If you could know what maintaining these appearances cost you might be surprised.

My capricious interior.

Falling away, I remain close.

～ Wild Heart

It is so precarious, day after day,
these inner desires, meltings,
flames.

❧ The Mirror I Don't Want to Hold Up

I am trapped in my own fears, sometimes they disperse and vanish like fog in the sun when confronted.

Like insects fleeing the light in the night on the counters of an old kitchen, scuttling, hissing.

❧ Insomnia

When I obsessed about writing the way I do a lover, I stopped sleeping. Now I keep my notebook with its empty white sheets beside me to write blindly in the night with a pencil without looking.

Words that flow in the symbolic between the imaginal and the real.

Reflecting and shaping.

All day, euphoric and tired,
such nights of intense love-making.

∾ *Sea-breaker*

It was a small sea-breaker, *Monsieur.* But love flowed over it.

An ocean of love that could not be
held back.

∾ *Wonder*

What carries us though?

How do we rise each day
so agility?

I'm not sure how I breathe,
eat, walk, see or hear, how my heart beats,
or write my way through
this story.

What is talent? What is the muse?
Why do we have to make art, create
businesses, produce culture, perpetually
shape our world?

This morning you are too far
away to share in this conversation
of wondering.

∾ Transparency

Monsieur, after an event, trip, workshop, conference, when you say, let's just be friends, or let's take a break, or suddenly stop writing erotic notes, it is clear you are elsewhere, pursuing.

How can you not see the transparency?

With your desire for encounters, I offer no complaint to your pursuits and conquests.

When it ends I may not be here, but that's a risk you always take.

You are a good man, *Monsieur*, and you love me.

In your absences, I don't stop loving you.

∾ Explore

Explore configurations of desire
in a world of mutable
connections.

∾ Glare

Shades of love
in an over-bright world.

Is love found, ever,
in the glare?

∼ *Possessive*

Monsieur, stop! I have never laid
claim to you.

No, I've never said, *mon homme, mon amour, you're mine.*

What a strange idea, *Monsieur!*

Impermanence rules.

∼ *Sand*

At the seashore she shouted incoherently to herself and flung handfuls of
sand into the air.

Sand from a beach so white it was like the pause between paragraphs.

∼ *Horizon*

I wanted to make it over the event horizon,
to get past fantasy to the real.

But I couldn't.

∼ *Wind*

In the angry, cold wind at the bus stop sand blows.

My eyes well; the world of bright sun, unfocused.

When I step on the bus, my collar, wet with tears. The bus driver,
concerned, 'How are you this morning? It's cold.' 'Yes, and that high wind
blew sand into my eye - I'm not crying.'' He closes the door and pulls the
bus into the traffic.

～ Nomad

You are a floater, tumbleweed, a fellow nomad.

How could it be any different?

～ Tracks

The tracks, where the switcher is.

You pulled it and we separated;
or, you went off elsewhere.

Gleaming steel,
it frightens.

The train yard,
a terrible vision
of the conventional.

I am responsible
for the manoeuvre
that caused the
track switching.

The trains sometimes run beside the ocean and she was there, skeletal,
antique black lace gown, shrieking,
flinging sand.

You said all your women are possessive
and you had to hide them
from each other.

∿ Joust

Monsieur, what you are suggesting is unexpected, and breaks all the rules of jousting.

Deleuze knows: we cannot be anything other than rhizomatic nomads.

∿ Switchboard

I sit at the switchboard, connecting people, transferring calls.

All day I do this.

∿ Operator

I re-route incoming calls—a relay station, transducer, the moment of crossing, transference. A voice of welcome, and connection. I am meaningless in myself. Only an operator of the switchboard.

Disembodied voices, friendly, or demanding, asking to be passed onto what or whoever they are looking for: a department, an individual.

What are the connections behind the connections? They are like nomads. I send them on their way.

The ring, the name, the extension, then silence as the voices move elsewhere, beyond the range of hearing.

At the desk I find myself wondering, *Monsieur*, if you came to me so I could re-direct you elsewhere.

∼ Blessing

On that day, the light bathing the world was visionary. The sun shone with determination against the cold. I shiver in your arms. We stand in the weak winter light, receive its lucent blessing. Even when the earth tilts and we are far away.

In your embrace, I am illumined.

∼ Threat

Everyone is a threat; she battles everyone,
without exclusion.

∼ Escape

Monsieur, you became a place of chaos in me.

I didn't know if we could continue. When you left it was okay because none of the difficulties had to be faced.

We are always escaping each other.

∼ Fragments

I wish to write a conventional letter of love, *Monsieur.* But all I manage are fragments and too many questions on the nature of love.

∼ Writing

A simplicity of surface
suggests deeper structures.

≈ Tides

Monsieur, you are a flux,
a vision of pulsing light,
the moon's tides
lapping on the shore
or vanishing on the horizon.

You come and go,
free, this motion,
our hearts open as the air
breathing over the world,
the rushing wind.

≈ Sores

Her lips, swollen with open, blistering cold sores.

She turned her crazed, cold eyes, "If I have to suffer these horrible sores,
why shouldn't you?"

And she kissed me.

I was a child.

Her black hair harsh against her white powdered face and the red greasy
lipstick.

❦ *Eyes*

Eyelashes against the halos refracted by the light on my reading glasses.

Eyes that see.

Eyes that weep.

Eyes that can never see themselves,
except by reflection.

Only other eyes, the anonymous gaze. Unless we can weep at the stranger's
or our own pain, tumult, accident, enslaveries, what are we?

❦ *Uncoiling*

In all the corners and crevices of the room
coiled spiral mazes
rainbow serpents.

Coiling and uncoiling
like rings
on my fingers and toes.

∿ *Muse*

Medusa is my muse,
and her snakes appear everywhere.

❧ Subjectivity

Our portrait, a self-reflection, who we are in our mirror-image, subjects *becoming-still*, petrified, turned-to-stone, we are art, despite temporal pulsations, that we are aging, changing

...as Medusa trails off, her head of hissing hair.
She cannot gaze upon herself.

We, subjects who
cannot behold ourselves.

❧ Inscribe

...the soft slip of flesh etched in
stone under the writer's hand.

◇ Chthonic

Soft cotton sarong, in wide swarths of orange, plum, cream and simmering moons, became a snake with many eyes. I know by the way it winds around my neck while I sway on the floor.

Serpents of protection.

Do I hallucinate?

Gold snakes cling, pour over my swaying arms, wrap around my curving belly as I shimmy and gyrate, the sensuous rhythms of flute and sitar.

I am possessed. The writhing waterfall of coppery snakes stream while I hold earth lightning in my hands like the Minoan Snake Goddess. I can't stop dancing. I writhe and undulate and spin like a whirling wind, a belly dancer, a dervish, a dakini.

I am the lady of serpents.

Everywhere they slither and coil, an energy of creativity that persists despite inner dissensions, the envy of the other.

The face of envy on the dance floor is a mass of dry, dead hair, an austere, thin frame, a rigid torso without sensuality, or warmth, the cruelty exposed. Its breath re-inhaled, the fumes. Unable to prevent. Incapable of damaging. Useless flap of useless motion. Rendered impotent, powerless.

Today the dictator died; the despot is deposed.*

The cries and laughter of freedom rise to the skies.

---

* Pinochet, the dictator who ruled Chile from 1973-1990, when many thousands were murdered, disappeared, interned, tortured, died in December 2006.

Writing

Let writing be writing.

Can words shape themselves to our experience?

Hesitancy

What position doesn't fluctuate? If the real is what returns to itself, can I? Can I stop the constant shifting, my heart, my muse.

Monsieur, I cannot flow in one direction. I contradict myself. Potent feelings flow in opposite directions, collide, aren't neat, contained, tidy or even explicable. While I would like to not be confused, unsure, to fight only my own fears, I am a storm of paradoxes.

Always departing, never arriving.

Can writing write impossibility?

We curve and sway in a dance of intimacy. A single flower, *padma lotus*, whiteness, of a spectrum of prisms, following an inner light, its lightning, even as the moon's tides surge in us.

It happened in the quietness of the moment.

Afterwards, enwrapped, a peace that lasts for days. Then the breaking, chaos swirls over.

There is a way through, even with resisting what we are approaching, pulling away, succumbing, falling back. Even with the red and white blossoms that perhaps notice us or not, roses of love with baby's breath in the pale blue art deco vase on the table beside the nightlight. Even in the cramped place with roots behind the walls that we can't see, on the soft pale cream sheets. In reciprocity.

➣ Haunting

In the configurations of our desire for the beloved other, what we imagine is how we appear to them.

Without the reciprocal, we find ourselves being haunted by a spectre, a vision that has no rootedness, that cannot flourish.

The spectral must be shattered.

Relinquish the haunting.

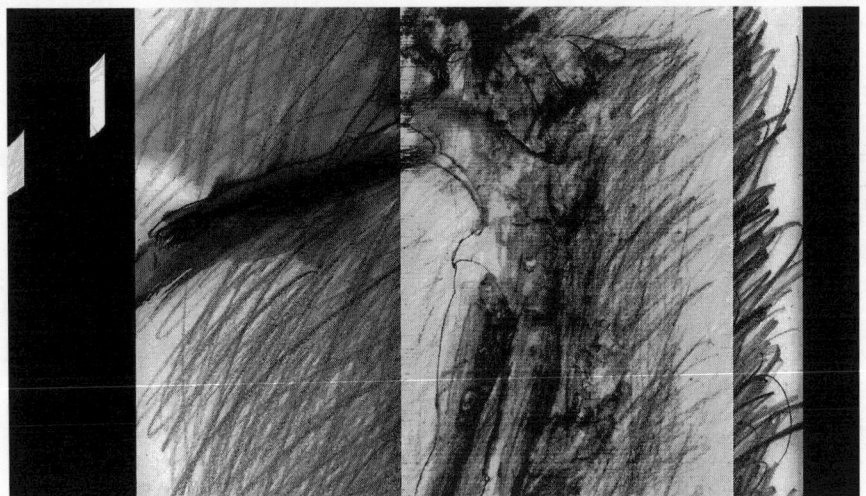

∽ Curse

On that day, on the dance floor, dark energies.

Tumours of anger metastasize.

Dancing rebellion.

Our dislike of each other. We grate, irritate, think dark thoughts about each other.

Malignancies broil into our dancing. Moving with a stranger, an innocent partner. I begin shouting at her.

She is flinging seawater and it is wetting me far inland in the dance studio.

From my loosened jaw, strings of curses sting the air. My fury strong. No-one should have to withstand this.

Around and around my dance partner I dance like a wicked woman. It is her turn to curse. She screams, then I do, but not at each other. Eventually, it subsides.

We come to see divine immanence in each other's eyes.

～ Target

Surf pounds in my ears.

Air hits me under her closed fists.

She is behind me, cursing. Her black habit sweat-soaked, hanging, stringy shreds. Her lipstick smeared; the red paint on her toenails cracked. She attacks.

She is upon me, the air from her fists on my back. When I turn surprised and see what is oncoming I move quickly behind her and whisper her favourite word, "Disgusting."

She shrinks back,
her target gone.

She shrinks back, blanched, withered, pocked bone, shredded muscle, porous skin, pulsing blood vessels, dull eyes.

She shrinks into a stiff board of rigid, repetitive motions. Unable to comprehend her lack of power.

She implodes.

I am free.

～ Touch

In the steam, you disappear. *Monsieur*, I feel your presence only by knowing. You sit before me until you vanish; hot clouds dissolve us into vapour. Your strong sensuality, like Zeus, yet you become a phantom. Until I am alone. When the hot breath of air presses in on me your hands rest on mine, our knees touch. Two figures of naked skin streaming as the steam subsides. It was in the room you built, this womb of steam from which we emerge wet and hot into the cold air of the welcoming night.

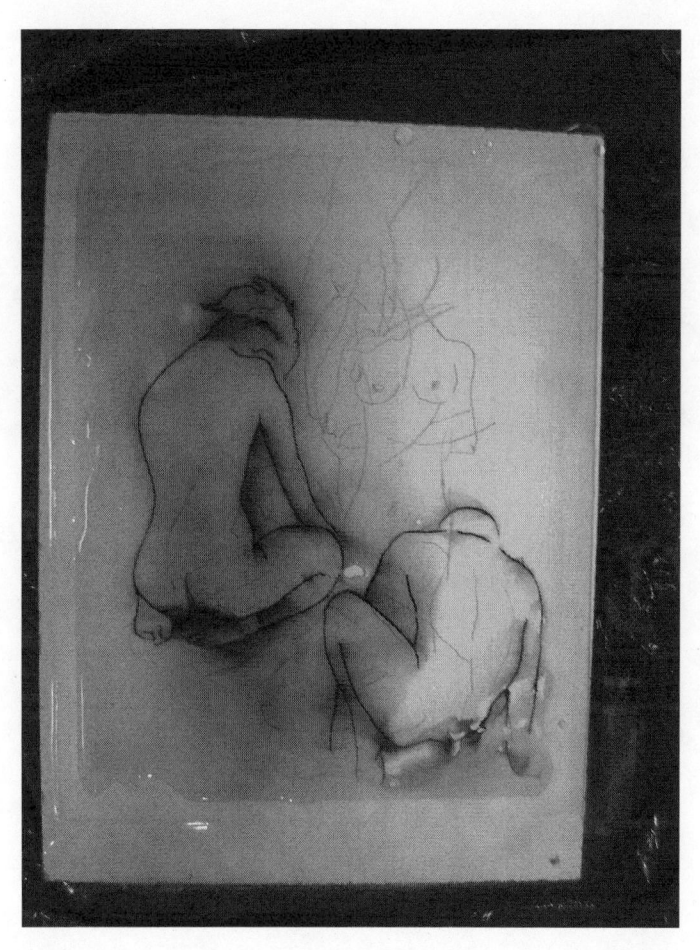

～ Rapture

Unfolding
through water
our bodies of rapture

streaming the truth of
the night sky, its melting snow.

An offering
to fire and transparency.

In the hot springs clouds uncover
a full moon of the New Year
you plunge into me
dance in the water
surging, volcanic.

Waves of heat
absorb us

into an immensity that has no name.

A writing of love,

transfigured.

～ Rupture

Do we imagine the depths of each other
differently?

Were we Shiva and Shakti dancing?
Our own *Sex and Lucia*
under the moon in the water?
You kiss my breasts as I float
before you, I massage your floating
rapture,
and how many times do we
undulate?
How continuously
do we hum ecstasy
in the silence of the winter's night?
Your final surge
rising, fertile, flowing
light, filling the lucid
darkness,
honey of
delirium.

We offer each other
pleasure.

The next day,
driving me home, you said
you wanted to be clear,
that you love me
but weren't in love
the magic of transformation,
absent.

~ *Portal of Breath*

There are words I must speak, though surely never will. You call me across the expanse. I kiss your closed eyelids. I lie over you softly, breathing with you. With each wave of breath, like sea foam, I cover you with a silent resounding mantra, I love you. Even while you call me to you, you do not hear the rippling of my heart. It is when you are asleep and I lie with you that I hear the fullness of the silence between your breaths. You are the full intoxicating sea-garden in repose and I am calmly delirious in the scent of the night. In the morning you have forgotten everything; even the savouring. How do we "translate the silence of the real encounter between the two of us?"*

---

* Clarice Lispector, *The Stream of Life*, trans. by Elizabeth Lowe and Earl Fitz (Minneapolis: University of Minnesota Press, 1989), p.43.

~ *Truth*

A year after
my abrupt absence,
the letter from
one of your lovers
about your nights with her
filling the hours
around ours, and the others.

Denials thrash
sea waves.

Blood-green
words scrawl in the sky.
Her teeth mottled, her white skin,
the cruel laughter
of gulls
scavenging
the beached creature.

What else
could you do, the birds flying seaward
but screech
lies.

Love was never
a question.

~ Relation of

Monsieur, it's not possession.

We can only come into a relation of openness.

You leave, and yet always return.

~ Distance

I spin away, her frothing mouth, icy wet black wool coat flying in the wind, the cold beach, gulls screeching overhead.

Her red scarf flies into a wind the colour of seaweed, *virid* and *cinnabar*.

If I am absent, she cannot
grasp me.

~ Reciprocity

A delicate exchange of sensibilities, sensitivity to the other, a flow back and forth, a *Tao*, giving, receiving, the mystery of encounter, is this possible, *Monsieur...*

with our capricious natures?

Does love allow us
to become who we are
and what we wish to be?

Can the reciprocity of our bodies of rapture
find reciprocity in our hearts?

Mon amour.

Can love
liberate

us?

~ Night Blossom

why should a flower not blossom at night

because the sun is swallowed by darkness

PLATES

～

All artwork is by Brenda Clews

1. Cover—Ink Drawing, 2014, 11.5" × 16.5", India ink, Moleskine sketch-book.

2. Polarity, 2014, 18" × 24", water soluble graphite, Noodler's ink, InkTense pencils and blocks, archival paper.

3. Braille, 2006 and 2012, charcoal sketch inverted and made into a poem painting.

4. Parchment Figures: Doubles, Doppelgängers, Clones, 2010-2013, 24" × 30", oil, acrylic, gold leaf on stretched canvas.

5. Three, On The Edge, 2012, 20" × 16", mixed media, 90lb archival paper.

6. Woman Seated, Waiting, 2012, 16" × 20", graphite, India and acrylic inks on stretched canvas.

7. Old Woman of the Sea, 2011, 14" × 15.5", India ink, conté crayon, oils.

8. Photograph of the author with the reflection of the painting, "Prostrations," in 2006.

9. "Every Angel is terror. And yet,
    ah, knowing you, I invoke you, almost deadly
    birds of the soul" from Rilke, 2nd Duino Elegy,
    2012, 18" × 24", charcoal, acrylic, primed canvas sheet.

10. Enfolded Luminosities: 'Prostrations,' 2006, 9 ¾" × 12 ¼" mixed media on Arches watercolour paper.

11. "LANGUAGE IS THE CAGE THROUGH WHICH I EXPRESS MY PASSION", 2011, 8" × 11.5", India and acrylic ink, gel pen, oil paint, Moleskine sketchbook.

12. Monochroma #2, 2014, 11.5" × 16.5", India ink, Moleskine sketchbook.

13. Blind, 2012, 6" × 8", charcoal and watercolour on archival paper.

14. Secret Love, 2010, 13.5" × 7.5", India inks, sepia fountain pen ink, oil paints, watercolor pencils and water-soluble oil pastels on archival paper.

15. Woman, Breaking Free, Rising, 2015, 8.25" × 11.75", graphite, Prisma-color premier and Pitt pen permanent ink, Moleskine sketchbook.

16. Better Left Unsaid, 2012, 18" × 22", graphite on 90lb archival paper, image digitally finished.

17. Dance, 2014, 4" × 8", charcoal on canvas.

18. Coil of Koi in Dark Water, 2012, 8" × 11.5", Moleskine folio Sketchbook, multi-media.

19. 'perhaps the landscape isn't what we rest in, perhaps the landscape is a consequence of who we are,' 2006, 8" × 11", oil, India ink on archival paper.

20. When Art Converges, 2014, 9" × 12", permanent inks on watercolour paper.

21. The Woman Who Is Not Quite Effaced, 2012, 8" × 11.5", graphite, acrylic, gel pen, Moleskine sketchbook.

22. And Then, 2012, 20" × 16", mixed media, archival paper.

23. Dancer In Red, 2012, 8" × 11.5", graphite, India and acrylic inks, Moleskine sketchbook.

24. The Woman Who Is Not Quite Effaced, 2012, 8" × 11.5", graphite, acrylic, gel pen, Moleskine sketchbook.

25. Writing, 2014, 11.5" × 16.5", India ink, Moleskine sketchbook.

26. The Poet [or Artist] & Her Muse, 2012, 12" × 17", charcoal on primed canvas sheet.

27. Delphic Oracle, 2014, 11.5" × 16.5", India ink, Moleskine sketchbook.

28. Photo from my videopoem, The Dancer's Backskin, 2011, digital image.

29. An earlier stage in the painting, Enfolded Luminosities: 'Prostrations,' 2006, 9 ¾" × 12 ¼", mixed media, watercolour paper.

30. Figment, or what is departing?, 2012, 20.5" × 16", mixed media on 90lb archival paper.

Acknowledgements

Tidal Fury was written during an inspired few months of intense poetry writing a decade ago when I was working full-time and was a single mother of two adolescent children. I wrote during coffee and lunch breaks, on the subway, in the late evenings at home. At the time, I was part of a network of poets who blogged, and many of these poems found their first drafts in Rubies in Crystal*, my blog. I am immeasurably grateful for the conversations I had with poets around the world during the writing of *Tidal Fury*, and in particular would like to thank a number of poets for their brilliance and support during the inception of the pieces that compose this final collection: John F. Walter, Elissa Malcolm, Myna Alexandersdottir, Ira Socol, Richard Cohen, and Patry Francis, among many others, some of whom never revealed their real names. We were part of fertile, teeming communities of poetries that were streaming through us.

I am indebted to Michael Mirolla and Connie McParland for their support as publishers and to Michael Mirolla for his editing. He is a force in the Toronto and International poetry community and has done much to bring fine poetry to public attention. My dear friend Luciano Iacobelli, a fellow Guernica author, has been a staunch support throughout the editing and publishing process, and I thank him deeply. I would like to thank John Oughton for reading the manuscript and offering a short promo précis, and for his support as a well-published poet, friend and for the collaborations we have done. Gabriel Quigley appeared on the scene as Guernica's videographer and his reading of *Tidal Fury*, his understanding of the poetry, and his ideas for videoing a book trailer, have been amazing—many thanks.

Lastly, and most importantly, I would like to thank my two children, Adrian and Kyra, who simply accepted a mother who sometimes sat, staring at nothing with a pencil and notebook on her lap, who was often mute, busy in the silent ways of poetry, for their unending, deep love and support.

---

* 'Rubies in Crystal' refers to the Sufi classic, *The Rubáiyát of Omar Khayyám*, one of my father's favourite spiritual books—the rubies are red wine in a crystal glass.

About the Author

Brenda Clews' work explores intersections of writing, painting, and video-poetry. Poem fragments are written into paintings. Or a painting evokes a poem that is later written into it. She may dance a poem while wearing a mask that has emerged from a painting. She is a multi-media artist whose approach to a topic includes poetry, painting, theory, dance, recordings, and video. Clews' oeuvre focuses on the plethora, multiple callings, the obsessive muse, the prism rather than the spotlight, or on multiple spotlights. She writes: "Where else do you flee but into the many? How else do you combine yourself?"

While she has lived in Toronto most of her life, Clews is African-Canadian, and was born in a small mining town in Zimbabwe. She cites her early years spent barefoot, living in a compound of mud huts, with many wild animals and the wonderful Ndembu people, in the jungle of Kafue National Park in Zambia, for her deep resonance with the beauty, strangeness and brilliance of the tribal mind and the natural world.

She has two children, whom she raised mainly as a single mother. She has edited university textbooks, poetry and novels, written articles for newspapers, taught Kundalini yoga, done temporary office work, and dog sitting, while maintaining a reclusive lifestyle of writing and painting. She has a degree in Fine Arts from York University and abandoned a PhD in English Lit many years ago. Clews has had solo art shows at York University, Q Space and Urban Gallery, and been in many group art shows. She has two chapbooks, *the luminist poems* (LyricalMyrical Press, 2013) and *the Performance Poems* (Epopeia Press, 2016). A novella, *Fugue in Green*, will be published with Quattro Books in 2017. She hosts a monthly Poetry & Music Salon in various art galleries and libraries in Toronto.

Printed in July 2016
by Gauvin Press,
Gatineau, Québec